The
Space
Race

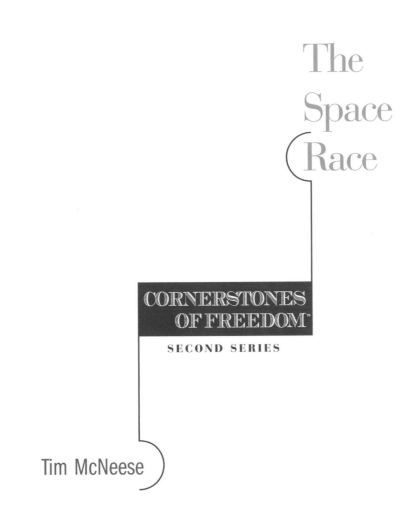

CORNERSTONES OF FREEDOM

SECOND SERIES

Tim McNeese

Children's Press®
A Division of Scholastic Inc.
New York • Toronto • London • Auckland • Sydney
Mexico City • New Delhi • Hong Kong
Danbury, Connecticut

Photographs © 2003: AP/Wide World Photos: 13 (NASA), 5 right, 20 right, 34, 44 top right; Corbis Images: 6, 11 top, 12, 18 bottom, 30, 44 top left (Bettmann), 20 left (Reuters NewMedia Inc.); Getty Images: 7; Mary Evans Picture Library: 4; NASA: cover top, 10 bottom, 21, 26, 27, 31, 36, 37 top, 40, 41 bottom, 41 top, 45 center; Photo Researchers, NY: 16 (NASA), 38, 45 bottom (NASA/SPL), 18 top (Novosti Press Agency/SPL), 5 left (Novosti/SPL), 10 top (SPL), 8 (SS), 19 left, 24, 44 bottom; Photri Inc.: 3, 11 bottom, 14, 19 right, 23, 25, 28, 32, 33, 37 bottom, 39, 45 top; Sovfoto/Eastfoto: 15 (Itar-Tass), cover bottom, 17, 22.

Library of Congress Cataloging-in-Publication Data

McNeese, Tim.
  The space race / Tim McNeese.
      p.cm.—(Cornerstones of freedom)
  Summary: Discusses the race between the United States and the Soviet Union to be the first nation to send a man into space and to land on the moon, including a glimpse of historical, technological, and human factors involved.
  Includes bibliographical references and index.
    ISBN 0-516-24201-6
    1. Astronautics—United States—History—Juvenile literature.
2. Astronautics—Soviet Union—History—Juvenile literature. 3. Space race—Juvenile literature. [1. Astronautics—United States—History. 2. Astronautics—Soviet Union—History. 3. Space race.] I. Title.
TL793 .M43 2003
629.45—dc21
                                        2002009028

1 2 3 4 5 6 7 8 9 10 R 12 11 10 09 08 07 06 05 04 03

On May 4, 1961, at the Cape Canaveral launch facility in Florida, the clouds drifted out over the Atlantic Ocean, and the launch team began a final countdown at midnight. At 2:05 A.M., on May 5, **astronaut** Alan Shepard, Jr., awoke in his dorm room at Cape Canaveral, showered and shaved, then ate a hearty breakfast. He put on his specially designed **space suit** and left for the launch site at 4:26 A.M. Less than an hour later, he climbed into the cramped **capsule,** a spacecraft designed to carry just one passenger. The sun began to rise on a clear, cloudless day, a day perfect for a space launch.

Throughout history, people have had many strange ideas about the moon. The ancient Egyptians told the story of Khons, the moon god, who lost an ancient board game against another moon god, Thoth. After that, he was not allowed to show all his light at once, but only a little at a time.

* * * *

At 9:34 A.M. the huge Redstone rocket's engines fired up. The rocket rumbled, shaking the tiny capsule at its tip and the human being inside. In less than a minute the spacecraft was zooming toward the heavens. Everything was going well. The men at mission control cheered for themselves and America's first astronaut. The craft streaked away from the earth. Two minutes later, the Redstone rocket's engine shut off, right on schedule. When Shepard returned to Earth, his entire flight had lasted only 15 minutes and 22 seconds!

THE SPACE RACE BEGINS

Throughout history, human beings have looked up at the Moon, the distant planets, and the stars with wonder. Later on, scientists began to acquire knowledge about these heavenly bodies. By the end of the 1950s, science and technology had advanced to a point where space travel had become a reality.

The first U.S. attempt to launch a man into space had been a success. Yet Alan Shepard was not the world's first space traveler. Just three weeks earlier, a **cosmonaut,** the Russian name for a space traveler, had flown in space.

✱ ✱ ✱ ✱

On April 12, 1961, Yuri Gagarin, a 27-year-old Soviet Air Force pilot, was rocketed to a height of 112 miles (180 kilometers) aboard a Vostok space capsule. Gagarin's trip had lasted nearly two hours, compared to Shepard's 15-minute suborbital flight, and involved a single orbit around Earth. When Gagarin returned from space, he boasted, "Now let the other countries try to catch us." The flight was only one of many firsts accomplished by the early space program of

LOOKING AT THE HEAVENS

Ancient civilizations held interesting beliefs about the objects they saw in space. Some thought the Moon was a god or goddess. Some Native Americans believed the Moon and the Sun were brother and sister. Some primitive people thought the Moon was a great, revolving ball of fire. Still others thought it was home to Moon demons or even great swarms of insects!

The Soviet Union's first space traveler, cosmonaut Yuri Gagarin, dressed in his space suit, sits in his *Vostok* space capsule before launch.

Wearing his silver-colored space suit, America's first astronaut, Alan Shepard, Jr., beams a smile from his seat on board his *Mercury* space capsule.

the Union of Soviet Socialist Republics (U.S.S.R.), a rival of the United States. The Soviet Union was the world's first and most powerful communist state.

THE COLD WAR

During World War II (1939–1945) the Soviet Union fought with the western democracies, including Great Britain and the United States, against Germany, which was led by the Nazi dictator Adolf Hitler. Together, President Franklin Roosevelt of the United States, Prime Minister Winston Churchill of Great Britain, and Premier Joseph Stalin of the Soviet Union made important strategic decisions. These

World War II map

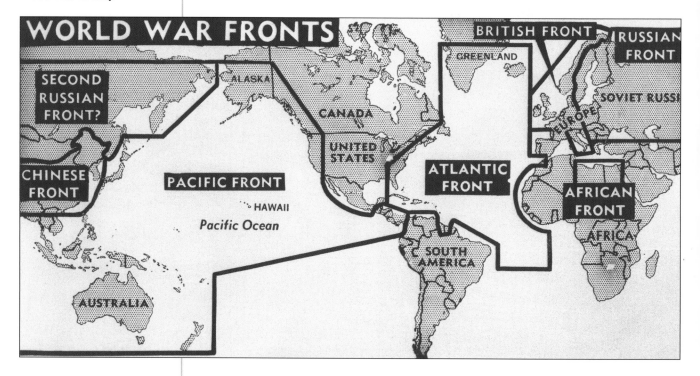

WORLD WAR FRONTS

SECOND RUSSIAN FRONT?

ALASKA

CANADA

UNITED STATES

GREENLAND

BRITISH FRONT

RUSSIAN FRONT

SOVIET RUSSIA

EUROPE

CHINESE FRONT

PACIFIC FRONT

HAWAII

Pacific Ocean

ATLANTIC FRONT

AFRICAN FRONT

AFRICA

SOUTH AMERICA

AUSTRALIA

Churchill, Roosevelt, and Stalin (from left) at the Yalta Conference in 1945 to discuss war strategy and postwar plans.

decisions not only determined the course of the war but the organization of the postwar world.

Once Germany was defeated, the wartime alliance broke down. What followed is known as the Cold War, a political, economic, and military rivalry between the world's capitalist democracies, led by the United States, and its communist states, led by the Soviet Union.

The Cold War was a struggle for power and influence around the world. In the late 1940s and the 1950s, it resulted in a series of tense conflicts. As the Soviets helped

Test detonations of such weapons as atomic and hydrogen bombs were carried out by both the United States and the Soviet Union during the Cold War.

create new communist governments in Europe and elsewhere, the United States attempted to block their efforts by sending foreign aid, including money, food, supplies, equipment, and even military assistance to those countries they believed were in danger of coming under Soviet domination. In 1948, when Stalin attempted to cut off western access to the German city of Berlin by a blockade, the United States

* * * *

and Great Britain carried out an airlift of food, medicines, blankets, and clothing to the people of West Berlin. When forces from communist North Korea invaded South Korea, the United States led the effort to stand up to the aggression, resulting in the Korean War.

An important part of the Cold War was the arms race, with both sides competing to create superior weapons. The United States developed the first atomic bomb in 1945, and the Soviets followed with their own bomb in 1949. In the 1950s the arms race centered on building rockets and missiles capable of delivering nuclear weapons. Throughout the decade, both sides improved their capacity to build and launch nuclear weapons. In June 1957 the Soviet Union successfully tested an **intercontinental ballistic missile** (ICBM). This new technology gave the Soviet Union the ability to launch a nuclear weapon against the United States. Already equipped with such technology, the United States found it important to constantly create new and superior weapons and delivery systems.

With the interest in rockets and missiles, space soon became an arena for Cold War competition. Who would control the limitless regions beyond earth's atmosphere? By the late 1950s the United States and Soviet Union were in a race to gain a strategic position in space. By the spring of 1961 the goal of the race was clearly stated. Just eight days after Gagarin's flight, President John F. Kennedy wrote to his vice president, Lyndon Johnson. He asked the

GERMAN ROCKET SCIENTISTS

During World War II, it was Nazi Germany that pioneered the use of rockets as weapons. When the war ended with Germany's defeat, the United States was eager to learn about and use this new technology. U.S. leaders also wanted to keep the Soviet Union from doing the same. To do so, they brought many of the leading scientists of the Nazi rocket program to the United States.

question: "Do we have a chance of beating the Soviets by [building] a rocket to go to the moon and back with a man?" When the question reached the top U.S. rocket scientist, Wernher von Braun, his answer was "yes." He said: "We have an excellent chance of beating the Soviets to the first landing of a crew on the Moon." For the next eight years, the two powers worked feverishly to develop the technology that would allow them to win the race to the Moon.

German rocket scientists, including Wernher von Braun, played key roles in developing America's early rocket and space programs.

During his first year as president, John F. Kennedy announced to the American people his goal of placing the first man on the moon before the end of the decade.

SATELLITES IN SPACE

In October 1958, President Dwight D. Eisenhower had created a civilian agency called the **National Aeronautics and Space Administration,** or NASA, to run the U.S. program. In the U.S.S.R., the Soviet military ran its space program.

The first space flights did not involve great distances or human beings in space. For Earth, space begins approximately 100 miles (160 km) above the planet's surface, where the atmosphere becomes so thin that a spacecraft can orbit

The National Aeronautics and Space Administration (NASA) was founded in 1958 by President Dwight D. Eisenhower.

Dressed for space travel, America's first seven astronauts pose for an official group photo. All seven joined the Mercury program as experienced military pilots.

FIRST ASTRONAUTS

The first U.S. manned space program was called Mercury. The original Mercury Astronauts, from left to right, were: (front) Walter Schirra, Jr., Donald "Deke" Slayton, John Glenn, and Scott Carpenter; (back) Alan Shepard, Jr., Virgil "Gus" Grissom, and Gordon Cooper. Deke Slayton was grounded in 1959 with a heart murmur and never flew a Mercury mission.

The Soviets' first manmade satellite, *Sputnik 1,* weighed only 85 pounds (39 kg). The satellite's four long, thin arms are antennas.

the planet at high speeds without the friction caused by flying through air. Such friction results in the aircraft overheating and losing speed. The first spacecraft reached an altitude just above this 100-mile (160-km)-high atmospheric barrier.

The Soviet Union fired the first shot in the space race in October 1957. That month, the Soviet Union launched the first manmade **satellite,** an unmanned device that orbits Earth and sends out electronic signals. *Sputnik 1* (the Russian word for "traveler") was a small, round aluminum object weighing 85 pounds (39 kilograms). It orbited the Earth and

* * * *

sent out a beeping signal. On November 3 the Soviets launched *Sputnik 2*, with a dog named Laika (Russian for "barker") onboard. Laika stayed in space for seven days. Unfortunately, *Sputnik 2* could not return safely to earth, and Laika died of heat exhaustion and a lack of oxygen. Even so, her experience proved that an animal could live in space. The launches of *Sputnik 1* and *Sputnik 2* greatly surprised many people in the United States and marked the true beginnings of the space race.

On January 31, 1958, the U.S. launched its first satellite, the 31-pound (14-kg) *Explorer 1*. The U.S. space program also used animals for space flight. Chimpanzees, pigs, rabbits, and hamsters were sent up and observed. Cats, rats, and mice also experienced the rigors of American space

Sitting on top of a large rocket, America's first manmade satellite, *Explorer 1,* is launched into space orbit.

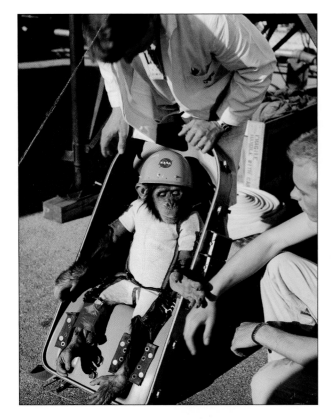

Animals bound for space, including this chimpaneeze, were given a variety of tests to determine their suitability for space flight.

A NOAH'S ARK IN SPACE

Sputnik 5 was filled with living things. The space capsule carried two dogs (named Little Arrow and Squirrel), a pair of rats, 40 mice, and 15 jars of fruit flies. It also contained plants, including spiderwort and chlorella. Samples of human skin cells were perhaps the strangest life form onboard. Scientists wanted to determine the effects of space travel on various forms of life.

flight. Soviet flights included more tests with animals, although a later flight, *Sputnik 6,* did not end well. That flight's two dog passengers were burned alive as the craft attempted to reenter Earth's atmosphere. Despite the failure of *Sputnik 6,* by 1960 Soviet scientists and military officials began planning for the launch of a human into space.

EARTH'S FIRST SPACEMEN

Training for space travel was difficult work. The stresses of early space flight included confinement in small spaces while traveling at high speeds. Space pilots had to be physically fit. In space they would experience weightlessness and, perhaps, extreme cold and heat. Weightlessness sometimes caused trainees inner ear problems that affected their sense of balance.

Astronauts and cosmonauts faced grueling training exercises. They were dropped into freezing lakes and placed in deserts to experience extremes of cold and heat. They worked underwater to simulate weightlessness. Trainees spent time in altitude chambers, breathing thin air. They

Several members of the original team of Soviet cosmonauts raise their hands together with the leader of the Soviet Union, Nikita S. Khrushchev (second from right).

were strapped into **centrifuges** that spun at great speeds like rides in an amusement park. There future space travelers experienced the crushing effects of high **G-forces**—pressure placed on the body by gravity, acceleration, and deceleration— that they would be subjected to during takeoff. There was always the risk of accidents occurring. In early 1961, a Soviet cosmonaut was burned alive while training in an isolation chamber. If such men and, later, women were going to face the extremes of space travel, their training would have to prepare them for anything.

In addition, astronauts and cosmonauts were highly trained in the sciences. They had to read thousands of pages of technical manuals and science books. They had to

THE SOVIET UNION'S FIRST COSMONAUTS

In May 1960 the Soviet Union selected its first six trainees for the Russian space program. All of them were military pilots. They were Anatoli Kartashov, Valentin Varlamov, Yuri Gagarin, Gherman Titov, Andrian Nikolayev, and Pavel Popovich. Only four of these original cosmonauts made it into space. Varlamov dislocated a neck vertebra while training, and Kartashov suffered a spinal hemorrhage while spinning in a centrifuge. Both men were removed from the program.

understand complicated physics and how to operate and repair all the elaborate equipment on board their various space capsules. Their jobs included thousands of details and hundreds of skills.

The space capsules themselves were simple, metal containers. They were placed on the tips of great rockets filled with thousands of gallons of explosive fuel. The capsules

Strapped in a centrifuge, an astronaut's face reveals the crushing effects of high G-forces as part of his training for space travel.

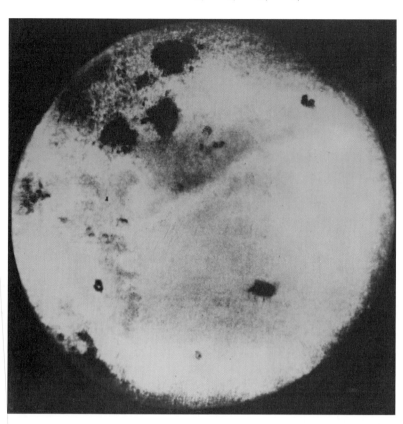

During the early years of the space race, the Soviets achieved several firsts, including shooting the first pictures of the far side of the Moon.

were filled with all sorts of electronics, dials, switches, and gauges, made up of thousands of separate parts. For example, the earliest Mercury capsules contained 7 miles (11 km) of electrical wiring! Even so, they were hardly big enough for one man to sit inside. With such complicated systems, equipment failures occurred on almost every flight.

THE SOVIETS TAKE THE LEAD

From 1957 through 1965, the Soviets set the pace of the space race. They launched the first satellite and the first animals into space. Gagarin was the first human in space. In addition, the Soviets took the first pictures of the far side of the Moon.

The Soviet space program included the first female space traveler, Valentina Tereshkova, years before NASA admitted women to the American space program.

They launched the first woman into space, Valentina Tereshkova. They launched the first spacecraft to carry two people, then the first to carry three. A Soviet cosmonaut was the first person to take a space walk, maneuvering outside a spacecraft in flight while attached by a tether.

But the U.S. space program did not stand still. Following Shepard, Virgil "Gus" Grissom was launched into space in July 1961. Then on February 20, 1962, onboard *Friendship 7*, John Glenn, a hero of World War II and the Korean War, became the first American to orbit Earth. He spent nearly five hours in space and orbited the planet three times. Glenn's flight proved a great inspiration to many Americans.

SPACE MARRIAGE

Sometimes, the space program brought people together in unexpected ways. Two Soviet cosmonauts married one another in November 1963. The first woman in space, the Soviet cosmonaut Valentina Tereshkova, married fellow space pilot Andrian Nikolayev. In 1964 Valentina gave birth to a baby girl named Yelena, whom people described as "the world's first space baby."

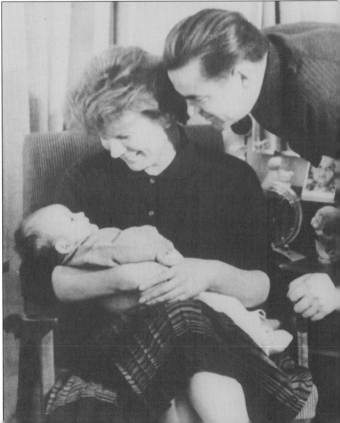

Tereshkova and Andrian Nikolayev with their baby.

In 1965, Astronaut Virgil "Gus" Grissom, one of the seven original Mercury astronauts, flew the first of the Gemini flights.

America's second astronaut in space, John Glenn, served as U.S. senator from Ohio from 1974 to 1999.

For the next several years, NASA continued its string of successes. In October 3, 1962, astronaut Wally Schirra, Jr., orbited Earth six times in nine hours onboard a space capsule called the *Sigma 7*. The next launch, in May 1963, was piloted by Leroy Gordon Cooper, Jr. Cooper's flight in *Faith 7* was the first to include a small television camera that sent video pictures back to earth while the craft was still in orbit. Cooper was so calm during the countdown of his launch that he fell asleep in his capsule. He even dozed off during his flight! But the unflappable Cooper remained in space for over 34 hours and covered about 600,000 miles (1 million km). The distance was more than would be required for a round trip to the Moon.

THE RECOVERY OF LIBERTY BELL 7

After astronaut Gus Grissom splashed down in the Atlantic in his space capsule *Liberty Bell 7* on July 21, 1961, the capsule began taking on water. Grissom was rescued, but the spacecraft sank 3 miles (5 km) to the ocean floor. In 1999, TV's Discovery Channel supported a recovery program, and divers found the capsule intact. It was rescued and placed on display in a museum in Kansas.

After resting on the Atlantic Ocean floor for nearly 40 years, divers rescued astronaut Gus Grissom's *Liberty Bell 7* space capsule from a depth of 3 miles (5 km).

American astronaut Gordon Cooper's 1963 Mercury flight onboard *Faith 7* went so smoothly that he sometimes fell asleep.

According to astronaut Cooper, from his position 100 miles (160 km) up, he could see boats, trucks, a village in the Himalayas, even smoke from chimneys. Despite some tense moments while returning through Earth's atmosphere, Cooper had enjoyed his ride in space. Traveling at such high speeds, Cooper was able to see 20 sunsets in only 34 hours! He later said: "I never tired of looking at the sunsets."

LAUNCHING THE GEMINI PROGRAM

Despite these U.S. successes, the Soviets continued to show the world what their space program could do when they launched two rockets, putting two cosmonauts into space at the same time. However, by the time the Mercury flights ended, the Soviets were beginning to lose their lead in the space race. Between June 1963 and October 1964, the Soviet Union did not launch a single space flight. With America's second space program, Gemini, preparing to launch its first spacecraft in the spring of 1965, the Soviets were desperate to put someone in space. An October 1964 flight called *Voshkod 1* carried three cosmonauts, but nothing significant was accomplished. One cosmonaut later described the flight as "simply a waste of time."

PRESIDENT KENNEDY'S TRAGIC END

In 1961, President John Kennedy had set the goal of the space race: To land a man on the Moon and return him safely to Earth by the end of the 1960s. But the president did not live to see that goal achieved. JFK was assassinated in Dallas, Texas, in November 1963. He did, however, live long enough to witness all six manned Mercury flights, the final one launching in May of that fateful year.

* * * *

But a second Voskhod flight, launched on March 18, 1965, did make space history. During the flight a thirty-year-old cosmonaut named Alexei Leonov emerged from his capsule through a collapsible air lock, an airtight compartment separating two places having different air pressures. The airlock was specially designed for a walk in space. While attached to the capsule by a 17-foot (5-meter)-long tether, Leonov hurtled through the void of space for ten minutes at 18,000 miles (29,000 km) per hour. The space walk came close to disaster when the cosmonaut's space suit ballooned dangerously, making it almost impossible for him to reenter the spacecraft.

While the space walk was a limited success, the **reentry** of the capsule back into Earth's atmosphere hit serious snags. Entering at the wrong angle, the *Voskhod 2* nearly

In 1965, Soviet cosmonaut Alexei Leonov made space history by making the first tethered walk in space. Leonov remained attached to his space vehicle by a 17-foot-long (5-meter) tether.

Gemini 12 was an unmanned flight used for terrain photography and testing equipment.

burned up and was 1,200 miles (1,920 km) off course when it landed. (While NASA flights landed in the ocean, the Soviets always came to Earth over land.) For a while, the Soviets did not even know where the craft was. Snow covered the ground at the capsule's location. When the capsule's parachute caught in some trees, the crew had to climb out, build a campfire, and pitch a tent to stay warm. When they were finally located, helicopter crews tried to drop warm clothing to the stranded crew. But the clothes caught in the treetops.

The first of the manned Gemini flights, the second series of launches carried out by the American space program, rocketed skyward in March 1965. Onboard were veteran astronaut Gus Grissom and a new space traveler, John

An American astronaut performs a tethered space walk. Astronaut Ed White took the first American space walk less than three months after the first Soviet walk in space.

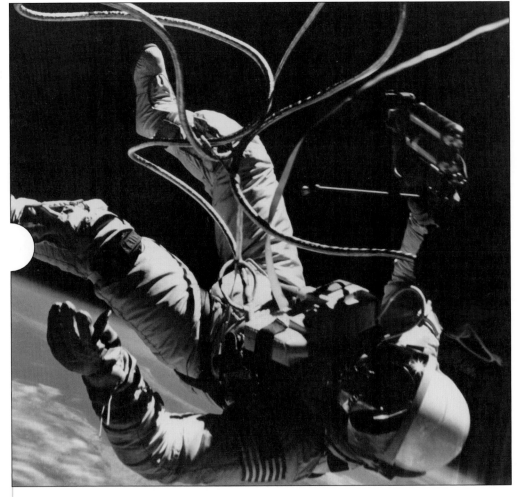

Young. The last Gemini launch took place in November 1966. There were a total of ten manned Gemini flights. One difference between the Gemini and Mercury spacecraft was Gemini's larger crew capsules, which could carry more than one astronaut.

Gemini astronauts experienced longer flights than Mercury pilots. They gained experience in space walks and with prolonged weightlessness. During the *Gemini 4* mission, astronaut Edward White II became the first American to walk in space. He was also the first man in space to use a hand-held device to maneuver his way around outside his Gemini capsule. Just two months after the *Gemini 4* flight on June 3, 1965, NASA launched *Gemini 5,* manned by former Mercury pilot Gordon Cooper and newcomer Charles "Pete" Conrad. Cooper and Conrad spent eight days in space and broke the former Russian record for the longest space flight. (The U.S. space program assumed a flight to and from the Moon would take eight days.) The final orbits of *Gemini 5* were so uneventful that the astronauts had time to listen to music broadcast from Earth, including the song "Fly Me to the Moon." On March 16, 1966, *Gemini 8* astronauts Neil Armstrong and Dave Scott connected their capsule with a target vehicle in space.

Charles Conrad was one of the first astronauts of America's second space program, Gemini, to experience space flight. He was onboard *Gemini 4* with veteran Mercury astronaut Gordon Cooper.

THE AMERICANS TAKE THE LEAD

By 1966 it appeared the United States space program was hitting its stride. The Gemini program was achieving its goals and setting new space records. NASA continued to launch successful ventures. Meanwhile, the Soviets

25

were beginning to lag behind. While the United States launched five flights in 1965, the Soviets sent up only one. In 1966 the Soviets launched no spacecraft, but NASA launched another five Gemini flights.

The five Gemini flights launched in 1966 included more **space rendezvous** (a space rendezvous is a maneuver in which two or more spacecraft meet in space) and additional space walks. From these flights NASA gathered essential information needed to send astronauts to the Moon. By year's end, the goal of launching a spacecraft to the Moon was closer than ever.

A camera onboard *Gemini 8* photographs a second U.S. space vehicle, *Gemini 7,* from a capsule window. During the flight, the two spacecraft docked together.

During the mid-1960s, both the United States and the Soviet Union launched several unmanned probes to the moon. Here, a photo captures the shadow of *Surveyor 1* as it makes a soft landing on the moon's dusty surface.

To help space scientists learn more about the Moon, spacecraft called **lunar probes,** designed to fly to the Moon and collect information, were launched. As early as 1959, the Soviets sent their *Luna 3* probe to photograph the side of the Moon that cannot be seen from Earth. On February 3, 1966, their *Luna 9* became the first spacecraft to land on the moon. That exploring craft transmitted photographs of the Moon back to Earth. Two years later, the Soviets sent up the *Zond 5* lunar probe. It made a complete orbit of the Moon and then returned to Earth intact.

The United States sent up its own probes. These spacecraft were called *Ranger, Surveyor,* and *Lunar Orbiter.* Between 1964 and 1965 three *Rangers* were launched toward the Moon. They took over seventeen thousand pictures of the Moon's surface. On June 2, 1966, *Surveyor 1* achieved a soft landing on the Moon. That probe took eleven thousand photos of the Moon's eerie landscape and transmitted the images back to scientists on Earth. The American probe *Lunar Orbiter 1* explored the dark side of the Moon in 1966, searching for a possible landing site for a manned spacecraft.

An aerial photograph shows a *Saturn V* rocket sitting on the gantry at the Kennedy Space Center. At 363 feet in height, the *Saturn V* was 60 feet (18 m) taller than the Statue of Liberty!

28

NASA INTRODUCES APOLLO

By the end of 1966 America's piloted space program was about to be launched. It was called the Apollo program. The goal: To land men on the Moon. It had been the goal of the American space program since President Kennedy had announced it in 1961. NASA determined that a giant *Saturn V* heavy-lift **booster rocket** would serve as the first stage of the spacecraft's launch vehicle, providing the tremendous initial thrust, or force, required to begin the voyage into space. The 363-foot (111-meter) *Saturn V* was 60 feet (18 m) taller than the Statue of Liberty! It would launch a spacecraft that was really two crafts. The **Command Module** (CM) would house three astronauts for six days on the journey to and from the Moon. Attached to its rear was a second craft, a larger **Service Module** (SM). This ship held the flight's fuel; **propulsion system,** the onboard system that provides a spacecraft with momentum or thrust; and the crew's oxygen.

The Soviets were still trying to find a way to the Moon, as well. By the end of 1965 the Soviets had approved a flight that would land two cosmonauts on the Moon. But the project's director died in January 1966. The new director was not as skillful in organizing the massive space effort, and plans had to be changed. By the end of the year the new plan called for landing one cosmonaut on the Moon. The Soviets tried to remain optimistic.

FIRE ON THE LAUNCH PAD

The Americans faced problems of their own. Design problems slowed Apollo's progress. Then the Apollo space

SPACEMEN ON TELEVISION

The space race inspired American television programming as well as scientists. In 1966, the NBC series *Star Trek* premiered. The series introduced characters who became household names: Captain Kirk, the alien Mr. Spock, and Dr. McCoy. The far-out series put the heroic TV spacemen in contact with "strange, new worlds." The campy space show did not resemble the real life space program in any way, but the series had a loyal base of fans and captured the imagination of the American public. After three seasons *Star Trek* was canceled. However, by 1979 a successful motion picture based on the original series reignited popular interest in *Star Trek*. Other movies followed, as well as another television series, *Star Trek: The Next Generation,* which aired from 1987 to 1994 and inspired several other series spinoffs.

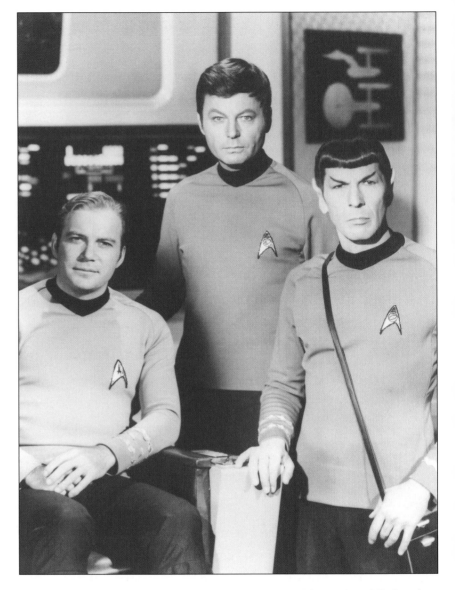

Actors William Shatner, DeForest Kelly, and Leonard Nimoy played Federation officers in the campy 1960s space travel series, *Star Trek.*

program faced its greatest tragedy. On January 27, 1967, the three-man crew of Gus Grissom, Ed White, and Roger Chaffee climbed inside their Command Module, which was sitting on the launch pad. They were supposed to run a full ground test of the space-craft. The fuel tanks on their rocket were empty, and no one expected any life-threatening problems during the tests. The astronauts' cabin was filled with pure oxygen. For nearly six hours the crew carried out several important tests. Then, at 6:31 P.M., Chaffee radioed the ground station's engineers: "Fire, I smell fire." Seconds later another message from the cabin: "Fire! We've got a fire in the cockpit!" Within seconds the space-craft's cabin was filled with intense heat followed by an explosion. All three astronauts died within minutes. The reason for the fire was never made official. The terrible accident put the American space program on hold.

A U.S. space capsule reveals the effects of the extreme heat created upon return into Earth's atmosphere during a space flight.

Meanwhile, the Soviet program continued to face difficulties. In late April 1967, the manned space module *Soyuz 1* had problems throughout its flight. Several onboard systems failed. Frustrated, the Soviet cosmonaut Vladimir Komarov at one point shouted "Devil machine! Nothing I lay my hands on works!" When he attempted reentry into Earth's atmosphere, the spacecraft plunged to Earth, killing the lone cosmonaut. With losses of life on both sides, neither the Americans nor the Soviets launched any men into space between April 1967 and October 1968.

BACK INTO SPACE

After the destruction of *Apollo 1* on the launch pad, the next two Apollo flights were canceled. *Apollo 4, 5,* and *6* were unmanned. Not until *Apollo 7* was launched on October 11, 1968, did American astronauts return to space. This flight included veteran Wally Schirra and two new astronauts, Donn Eisele and Walter Cunningham, flying onboard a redesigned Command Module. The astronauts performed a separation and rendezvous maneuver in space. For the most part, everything went beautifully during the eleven-day space flight. Unfortunately, Schirra developed a cold during the flight, which spread to his fellow crewmen. Afraid that, due to their colds, their eardrums would burst from pressure during reentry, the three astronauts became the first to return from space without their helmets on.

Within two weeks of *Apollo 7's* return, the Soviets launched an unmanned *Soyuz 2*. While the plan was for a cosmonaut to dock his craft, *Soyuz 3*, with *Soyuz 2*, he was unable to make the connection in space. But the Soviets were in space again, moving closer to the Americans. Word soon reached the Americans that the Soviets were intending to make a flight to the Moon as soon as possible. Immediately it was decided that *Apollo 8* would be a Moon flight.

The American space program experienced tragedy and setback in 1967 when an electrical fire swept through the airtight capsule, killing NASA astronauts Gus Grissom, Ed White, and Roger Chaffee.

As Florida palm trees sway from the impact, *Apollo 7* lifts off from its launch site at the Kennedy Space Center.

TO THE MOON

After an accident involving a Soviet proton booster, a rocket powerful enough to send a manned spacecraft to the Moon, the Russian space program again ground to a halt. This put the Americans in the front seat for the first Moon launch. Four days before Christmas, on December 21, 1968, astronauts Frank Borman, James Lovell, and Bill Anders were aboard *Apollo 8*. Burning 15 tons of fuel a second, a giant *Saturn V* rocket sent them aloft.

As *Apollo 8* made two orbits of the Earth, the astronauts checked all the onboard systems. Then, ground control gave the green light, and the spacecraft's third-stage motor revved to nearly 25,000 miles (40,000 km) per hour. Soon,

NASA engineers perform tests on the *Apollo 8* capsule. In 1968, astronauts Frank Borman, James Lovell, and Bill Anders piloted the capsule to the far side of the moon.

Apollo 8 was headed into deep space. During the flight the astronauts turned their TV camera toward Earth and beamed its image to mission control, located in Houston, Texas. As they entered the pull of the Moon's gravity, the crew increased the ship's **velocity,** or speed. They prepared to pass behind the Moon, out of sight of the Earth and out of radio contact.

For the first time, human beings would be completely beyond the reach of their home planet. Anders radioed to Earth: "Thanks a lot, troops. We'll see you on the other side." Thirty-five minutes later, *Apollo 8* emerged from the blackness. Once again, mission control could hear the astronauts' voices. Back home, Americans across the country watched their televisions as shadowy images of the Moon were beamed to Earth. With Christmas just days away, the astronauts read to those listening on Earth a passage from the Bible's Book of Genesis: "In the beginning, God created the heavens and the earth . . ."

After nine orbits of the lunar surface *Apollo 8* was ready to come home. The ship's main engine sent the spacecraft hurtling through space. Finally, the Service Module, no longer necessary, was released. The Command Module reached Earth's atmosphere and, at 34,000 feet (10,000 m), released the first of its parachutes. After *Apollo 8* splashed down, the astronauts were picked up by helicopter. The world's first visitors to the Moon had returned.

For the Soviets the success of *Apollo 8* represented a serious blow. Soon after the NASA flight to the Moon, the Soviet cosmonaut group in training for a Moon landing was disbanded. The American space program had knocked the wind out of the Soviet program's sails.

CHARLIE BROWN AND SNOOPY

By 1969 the American space program was preparing to launch a manned Moon landing. *Apollo 9* was launched in March with three astronauts onboard: Jim McDivitt, David Scott, and Rusty Schweickart. The flight's purpose was to test the Lunar Module, which the astronauts called "Spider." *Apollo 9* proved extremely successful.

For a while, NASA considered sending *Apollo 10* to the Moon for a manned landing. But the decision was made to wait and make certain everything was ready. The next NASA flight—piloted by Tom Stafford, John Young, and Gene Cernan—blasted off on May 18, 1969. Again American astronauts made their way to the Moon, orbiting in a

Astronaut David R. Scott steps outside of *Apollo 9* during the fourth day of the Earth-orbital mission

Command Module the astronauts named after the cartoon character *Charlie Brown.* The Lunar Module was called *Snoopy,* for Charlie Brown's pet beagle. The astronauts onboard *Snoopy* flew their Lunar Module to within 9 miles (14.5 km) of the Moon's surface. *Apollo 10* was a successful mission. The greatest achievement of the U.S. space program was less than two months away.

Three astronauts had been selected for the flight: Michael Collins, Edwin "Buzz" Aldrin, and Neil Armstrong, a former X-15 rocket plane test pilot. As the date for the Moon launch

Photographed from a window onboard *Apollo 10's* Command Module *Charlie Brown,* the Lunar Module, *Snoopy,* descends toward the Moon's shadowy surface.

Apollo 10 astronauts Gene Cernan, John Young, and Tom Stafford don baseball caps from the aircraft carrier USS *Princeton* after successfully completing their historic 1969 Moon flight.

approached, millions of people experienced "Moon Fever." By the mid-1960s the space program had became boring to many. Now, NASA once again became the center of the nation's attention. When *Apollo 11* and its crew lifted off on the morning of July 16, 1969, 600 million people watched the event on television.

"ONE GIANT LEAP"

Three days later, *Apollo 11* arrived in orbit around the Moon. Armstrong and Aldrin entered the lunar module, named *Eagle*. On board, they began to make their 69-mile (111-km) descent to the Moon's surface, a twelve-minute

Apollo 11 astronauts Neil Armstrong, Michael Collins, and Edwin Aldrin were the first human space travelers to reach the Moon's surface.

From a viewing section at the Kennedy Space Center, former President Lyndon B. Johnson (center of photo) watches the launch of *Apollo 11*, along with the country's vice president, Spiro T. Agnew (right).

ride down to a target landing spot called the Sea of Tranquility. Suddenly, alarms inside *Eagle* rang out, indicating a computer overload, but the problem was not serious. Like a giant metallic spider, the Lunar Module finally touched down on the dusty surface of the Moon. Astronaut Neil Armstrong informed all those watching from Earth: "Houston, Tranquility Base here. The *Eagle* has landed." It had been tense. After he realized the module was headed for the lip of a 40-foot-wide (12.2 m) crater, Armstrong had bypassed the ship's computer and manually landed the craft several miles away. When the module touched down, there was only six seconds of landing fuel remaining!

As Michael Collins orbited above in the Command Module, Armstrong and Aldrin put on special space suits for their visit to the Moon's surface. Hours later, Armstrong began climbing down an exterior ladder, with Aldrin guiding him.

In the powder dust of the Moon's surface, the bootprint of NASA astronaut Edwin "Buzz" Aldrin leaves a lasting impression.

Armstrong pulled a cord that released the pair's equipment, including a television camera that was attached to one of the Lunar Module's legs. The camera sent images of Armstrong back to Earth as hundreds of millions of people around the world tuned in to witness man's first steps on the Moon. Finally, at 10:56 P.M. (Eastern Daylight Time), Armstrong's astronaut boot left the ladder's bottom rung and stepped onto the surface of a world where no humans had ever walked. He then spoke the words heard from one world to another: "That's one small step for man, one giant leap for mankind."

Forty minutes later, Aldrin joined his fellow astronaut. They placed a small plaque on the Moon that read: "Here men from the planet Earth first set foot upon the Moon, July 1969 A.D. We came in peace for all mankind." The astronauts placed an American flag on the site. They received a telephone call from President Richard Nixon, who wanted to congratulate them. During their two-and-a-half hour stay on the Moon, Armstrong and Aldrin collected soil and rock samples. Then, covered in dust, the astronauts reboarded their Lunar Module. Twenty-one hours after it had landed, the *Eagle* blasted off. The blast knocked the American flag down into the Moon's powdery surface.

Days later, Earth's Moon men returned to their home planet, splashing down in the Pacific Ocean. The astronauts were tired and still dusty, but they were home. Americans from coast to coast were proud of their astronaut heroes and of their space program. NASA had accomplished the dream of President Kennedy. Only eight years had passed since the president had presented the grand challenge to his

During their two-and-a-half hour walk on the Moon, NASA astronauts Neil Armstrong and Edwin Aldrin plant the American flag.

nation's scientists, engineers, and space pilots. At last, the dream of human beings reaching toward the stars was no longer a dream. Instead, it had become another example of the potential of the human race.

COOPERATION IN SPACE

In the 1960s the United States and the Soviet Union competed with one another during their race into space. But by the 1970s, the two superpowers were cooperating on space flights. In 1975 America's *Apollo 18* and the Soviet's *Soyuz 19* docked together in space, allowing astronauts and cosmonauts to shake hands. On board *Apollo 18* was fifty-one-year-old Deke Slayton, the same space pilot who had been dropped from the Mercury program in 1959 for health reasons.

Three American astronauts—Deke Slayton, Thomas Stafford, and Vance Brand—pose with two Soviet cosmonauts, Alexei Leonov and Valery Kubasov. During a 1975 flight, the five space travelers docked their *Apollo 18* and *Soyuz 19* crafts together in space. Ten years earlier, Leonov had been the first man to walk in space.

41

Glossary

astronaut—American name for a space pilot

booster rocket—a launch vehicle's first stage, designed to thrust modules into space

capsule—the part of a spacecraft designed to carry a passenger

centrifuge—a training device featuring compartments that spin at great speeds

Command Module—the space compartment occupied by space travelers

cosmonaut—Russian name for space traveler or space pilot

G-forces—pressure placed on the body by gravity, acceleration, and deceleration. The force of gravity at the Earth's surface is 1 G.

intercontinental ballistic missile—a weapons system capable of firing a missile from one continent to another

lunar probe—an unmanned space vehicle designed to fly to the Moon and collect information

National Aeronautics and Space Administration (NASA)—the civilian agency established in 1959 to develop the American space program

propulsion system—the onboard system that provides a spacecraft with momentum, or thrust

reentry—the part of a space flight when a space vehicle descends into Earth's atmosphere

satellite—an object that orbits a heavenly body, such as the Earth. The Moon is Earth's natural satellite.

Service Module—the part of a spacecraft that contains the flight's fuel, propulsion system, and the crew's oxygen

space rendezvous—a space maneuver in which two or more spacecraft meet in space

space suit—a specially designed suit worn by space travelers

velocity—the speed of a moving object

weightlessness—lightness caused by a lack of gravity pulling the object down

Timeline: The Space

1957

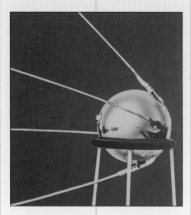

OCTOBER 4
The Soviets launch the first manmade satellite, *Sputnik 1*, into orbit.

1958

JANUARY 31
The United States launches the first American satellite, *Explorer 1.*

1961

APRIL 12
The Soviets launch the first man, Russian cosmonaut Yuri Gagarin, into space.

MAY 5
The first U.S. astronaut, Alan Shepard, Jr., is launched by *Mercury 3* into suborbital space onboard the space capsule *Freedom 7.*

1962

FEBRUARY 20
U.S. astronaut John Glenn, in *Friendship 7,* becomes the first American to orbit the Earth during the flight of *Mercury 6.*

1963

MAY 15
U.S. astronaut Leroy Gordon Cooper, Jr., aboard *Mercury 9,* takes the first TV pictures from space while still in orbit.

1964

MARCH 18
Soviet cosmonaut Alexei Leonov takes the world's first space walk in *Voshkod 2*

MARCH 23
NASA launches Gemini 3, the first of the manned Gemini flights. On board are Virgil "Gus" Grissom and John Young.

Race

JUNE 3
Gemini 4 is launched with astronauts James McDivitt and Edward White II. White takes the first space walk for an American.

FEBRUARY 9
Soviet probe *Luna 9* lands on the moon.

MAY 30
The U.S. launches an unmanned lunar probe, *Surveyor 1,* which sends back photos from the Moon's surface.

AUGUST 21
Astronauts Gordon Cooper and Pete Conrad fly *Gemini 5* and break the Russian record for the longest space flight.

NOVEMBER 11
The last of the Gemini flights (12) launches with James Lovell and Edwin Aldrin. The Soviet Union launches no manned space flights. By the end of 1966, NASA is prepared to launch its Apollo space program.

JANUARY 27
Three American astronauts die in launch pad fire: Virgil "Gus" Grissom, Ed White, and Roger Chaffee. As a result, the United States launches no manned flights during the entire year.

APRIL 23
Russian spacecraft *Soyuz 1* is launched with a single cosmonaut, Vladimir Komarov. Problems on board the spacecraft result in the death of the cosmonaut.

DECEMBER 21
Apollo 8 is launched with astronauts Frank Borman, James Lovell, and Bill Anders. The Command Module rounds the dark side of the Moon.

JULY 16
Three U.S. astronauts— Michael Collins, Edwin Aldrin, and Neil Armstrong— are launched to the Moon on board *Apollo 11.* Armstrong and Aldrin land on the Moon's surface and the two astronauts are the first men to walk on the Moon.

To Find Out More

BOOKS

Bay, Timothy. *First to the Moon.* New York: CPI Group, 1993.

Becklake, John. *Man and the Moon.* Morristown, NJ: Silver Burdett Co., 1981.

Charleston, Gordon. *Armstrong Lands on the Moon.* New York: Dillon Press, 1994.

Chester, Michael. *Let's Go to the Moon.* Revised edition. New York: Putnam, 1974.

Fraser, Mary Ann. *One Giant Leap.* New York: Henry Holt, 1993.

Stein, R. Conrad. *Apollo 11.* Danbury, CT: Children's Press, 1992.

ORGANIZATIONS AND ONLINE SITES

To make contact with the National Aeronautics and Space Administration (NASA) and ask questions, send an email to *comments@hq.nasa.gov* or send a letter to NASA Headquarters, Public Affairs Office–Code P, 300 E. Street SW, Washington, DC 20546.

Part of the official government website for NASA designed for kids *www.nasa.gov/kids.html*

Index

About the Author

Tim McNeese is an Associate Professor of History at York College in Nebraska. He is the author of more than fifty books on everything from Mississippi steamboats to the Great Wall of China. He grew up in the Missouri Ozarks, where he remembers watching early space launches on a black-and-white television with his classmates in the school cafeteria. Professor McNeese graduated from York College with an Associate of Arts degree, as well as Harding University where he received his Bachelor of Arts degree in history and political science. He received his Master of Arts degree in history from Southwest Missouri State University. As a writer for adults as well as children, he has earned a citation in the "Something About the Author" reference work. Professor McNeese is married to Beverly McNeese, who teaches English at York College.